Harmony's World of Friends

Holiday Edition

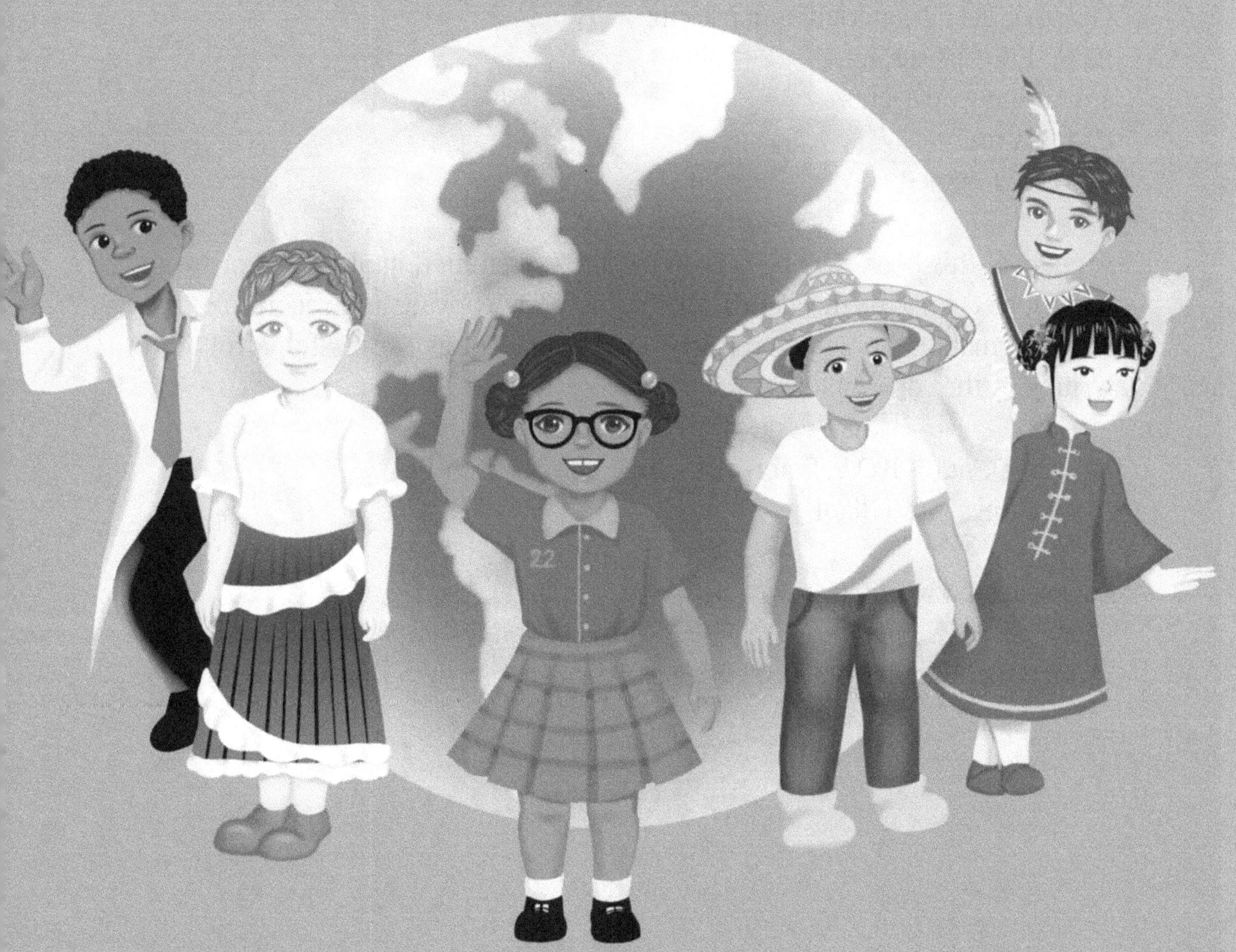

THIS COLORING BOOK BELONGS TO:

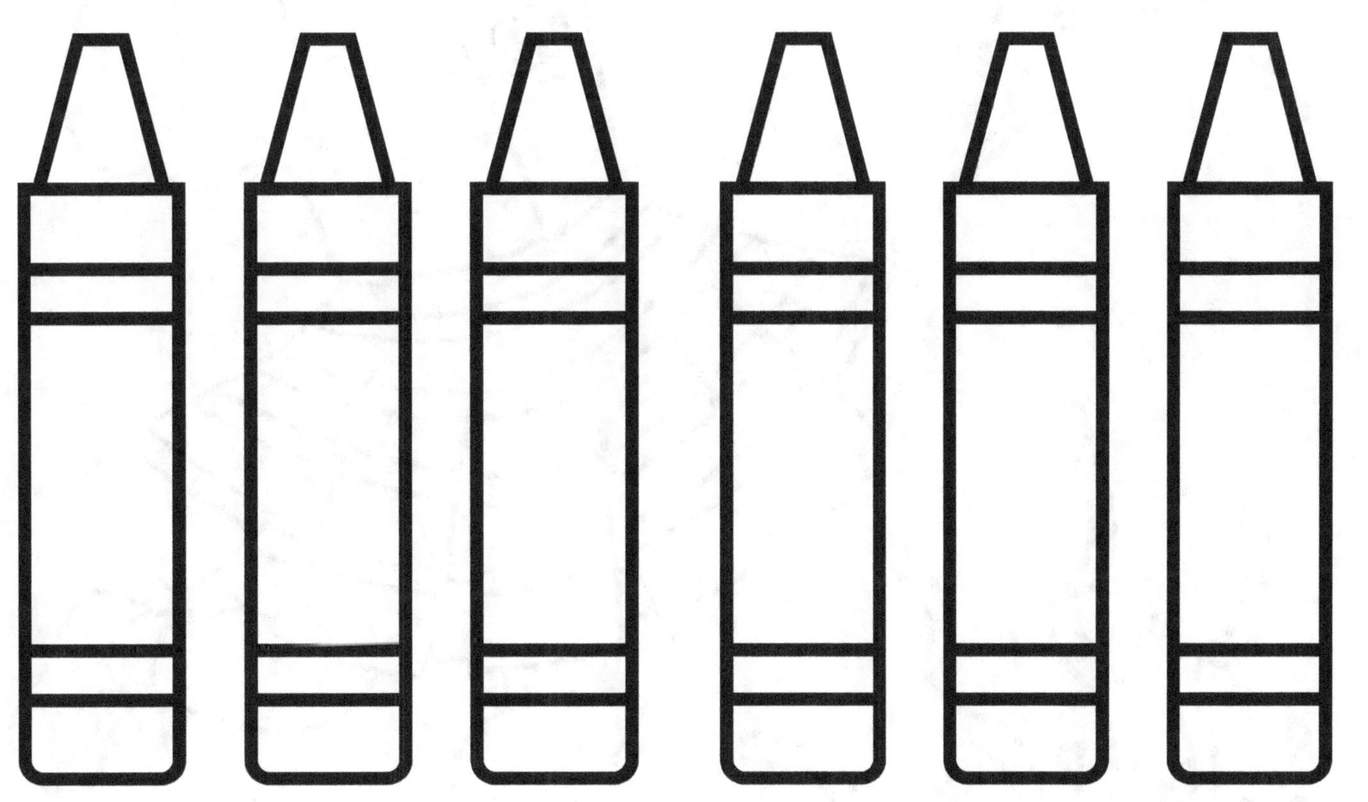

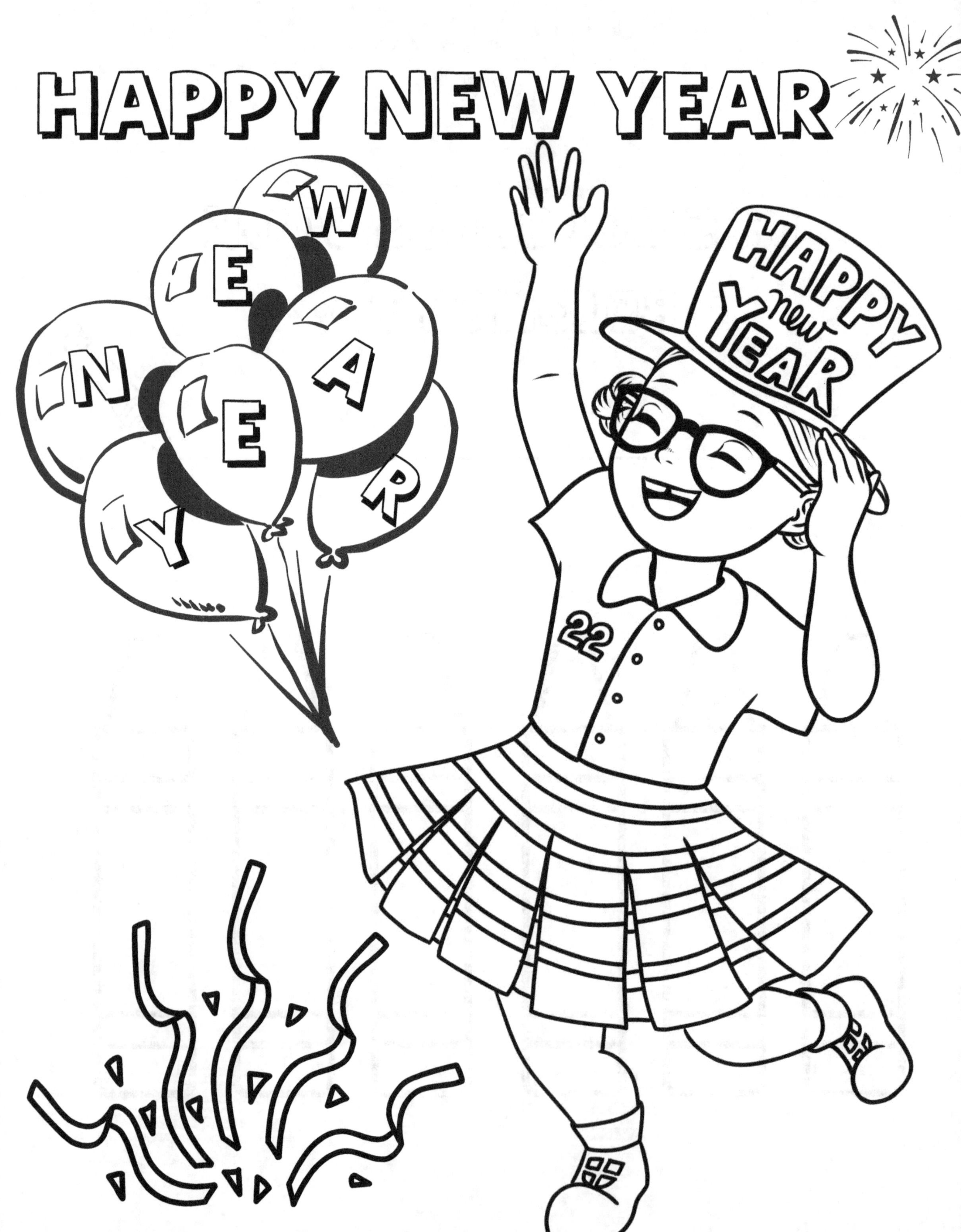

HAPPY NEW YEAR
N
E
W
Y
E
A
R
HAPPY
new
YEAR
22

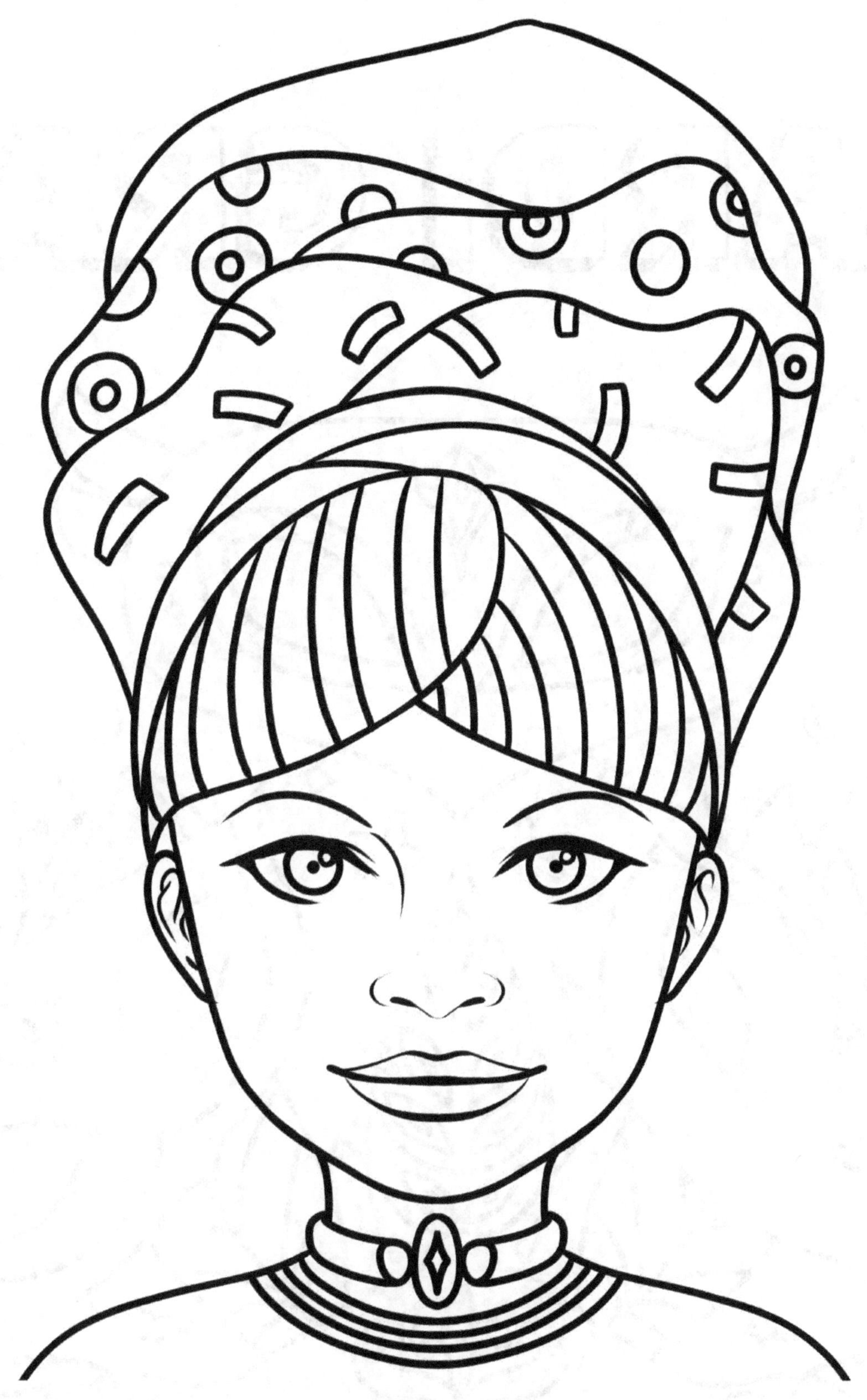

DANYELLE

MARDI GRAS

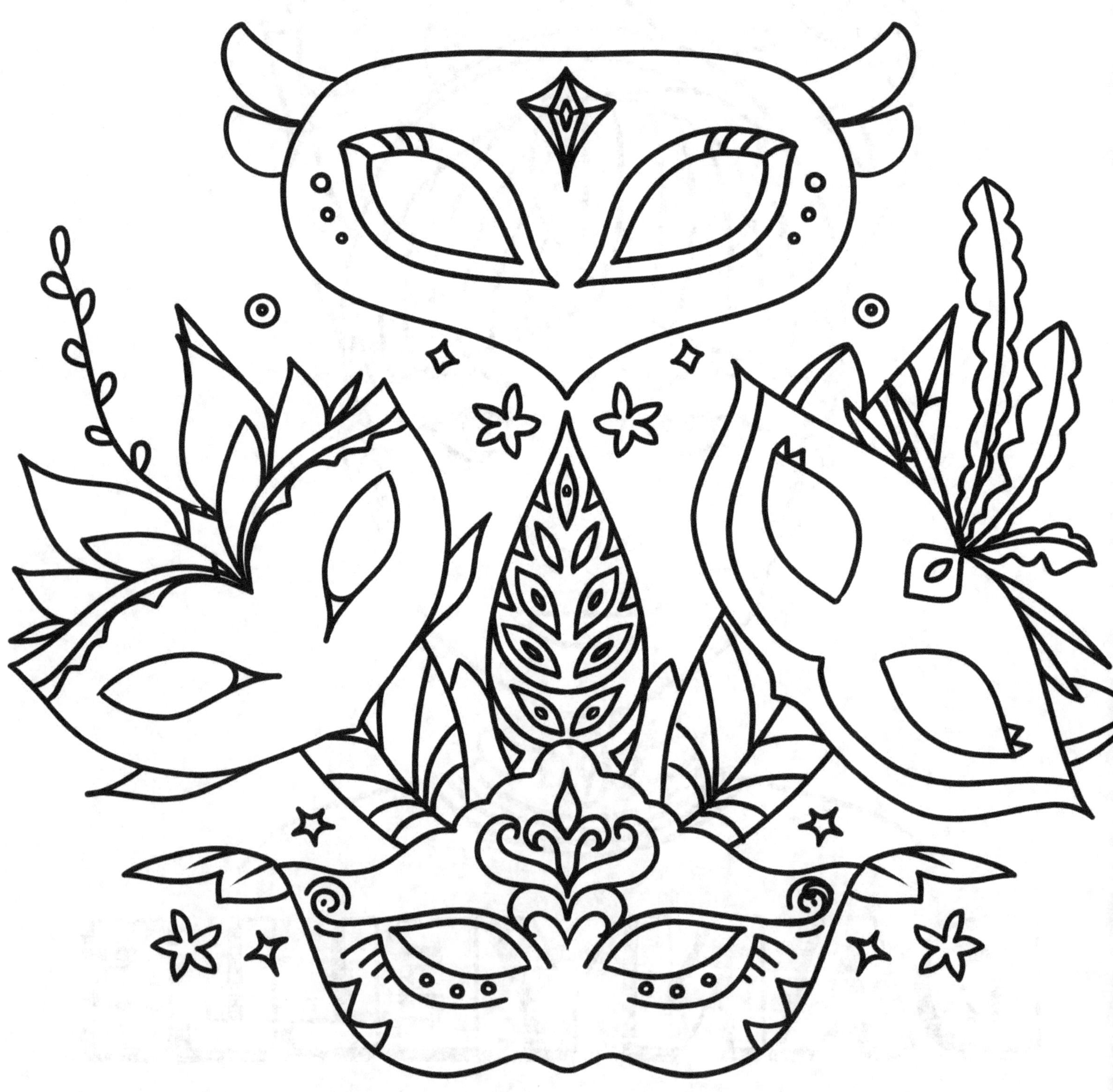

HAPPY EASTER

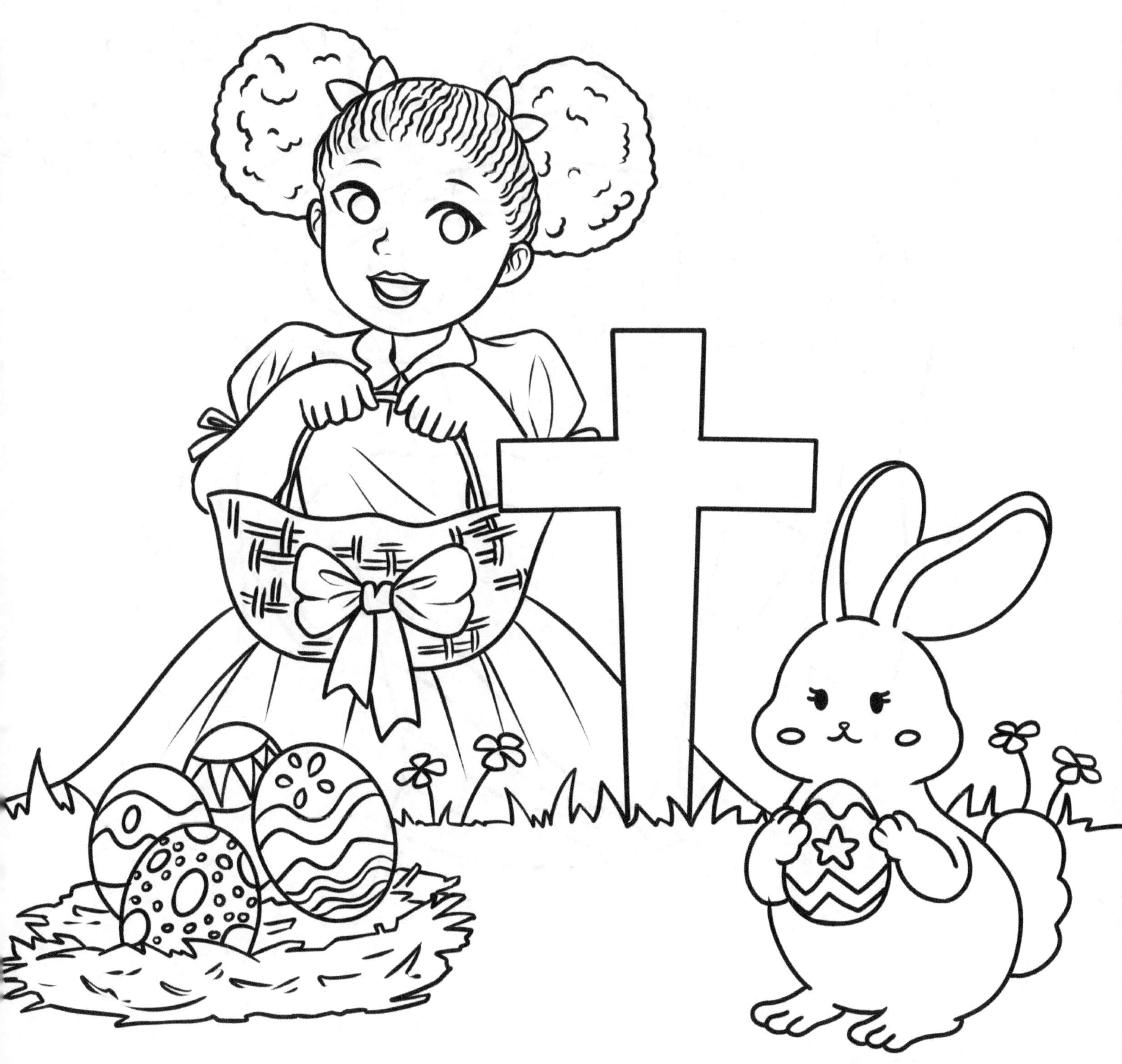

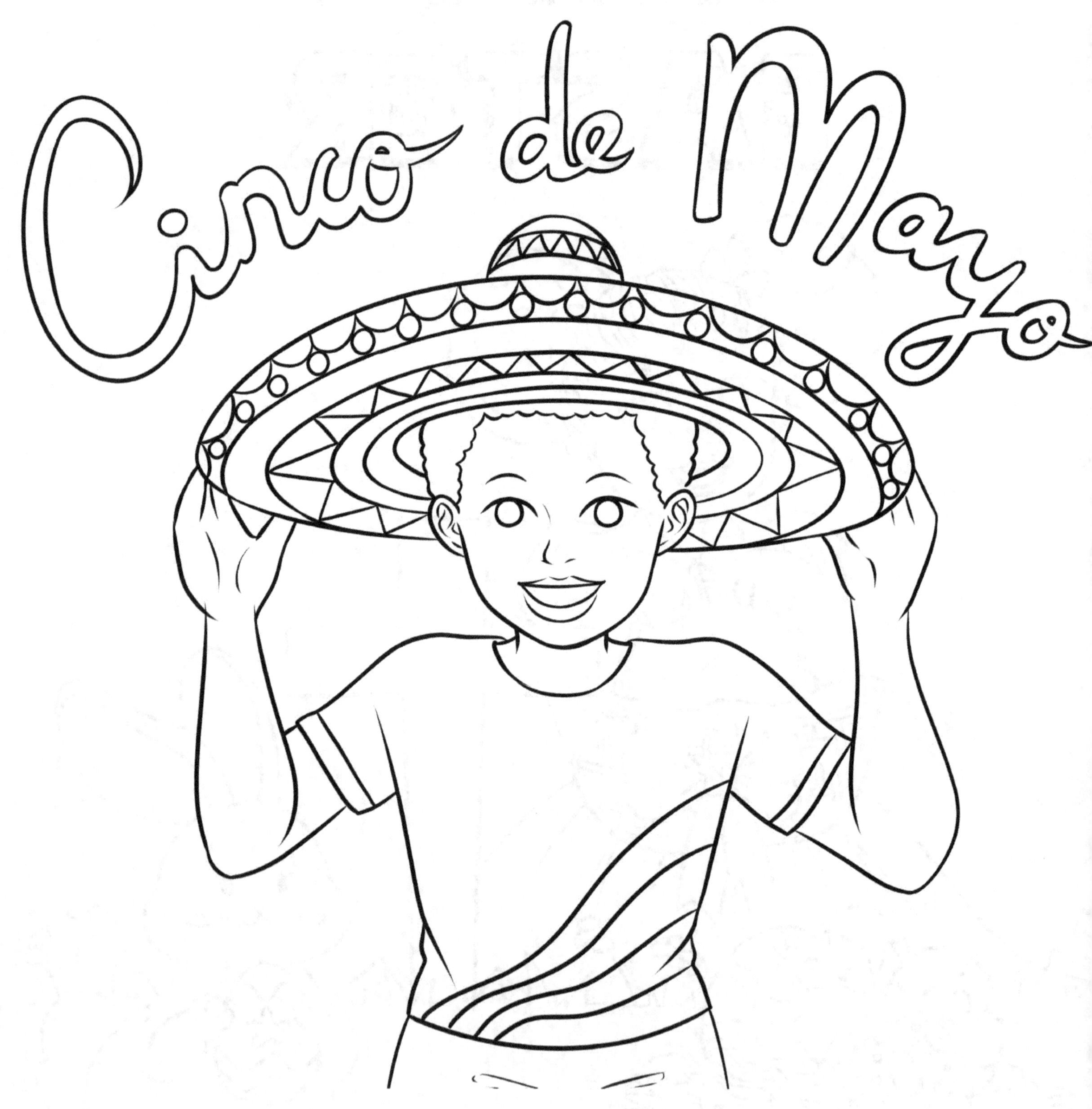

Cinco de Mayo

HAPPY MOTHER'S DAY

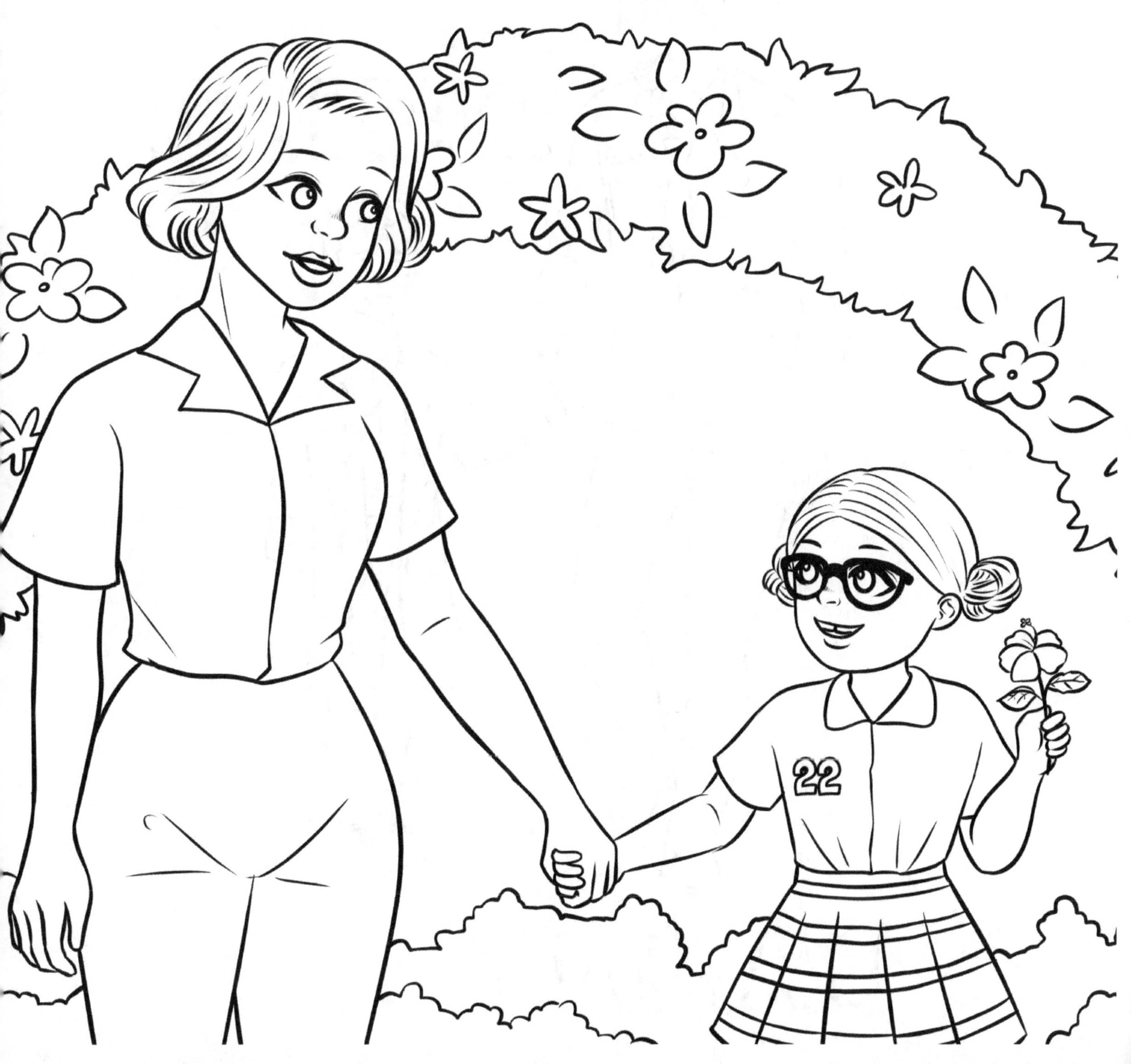

HAPPY FATHER'S DAY

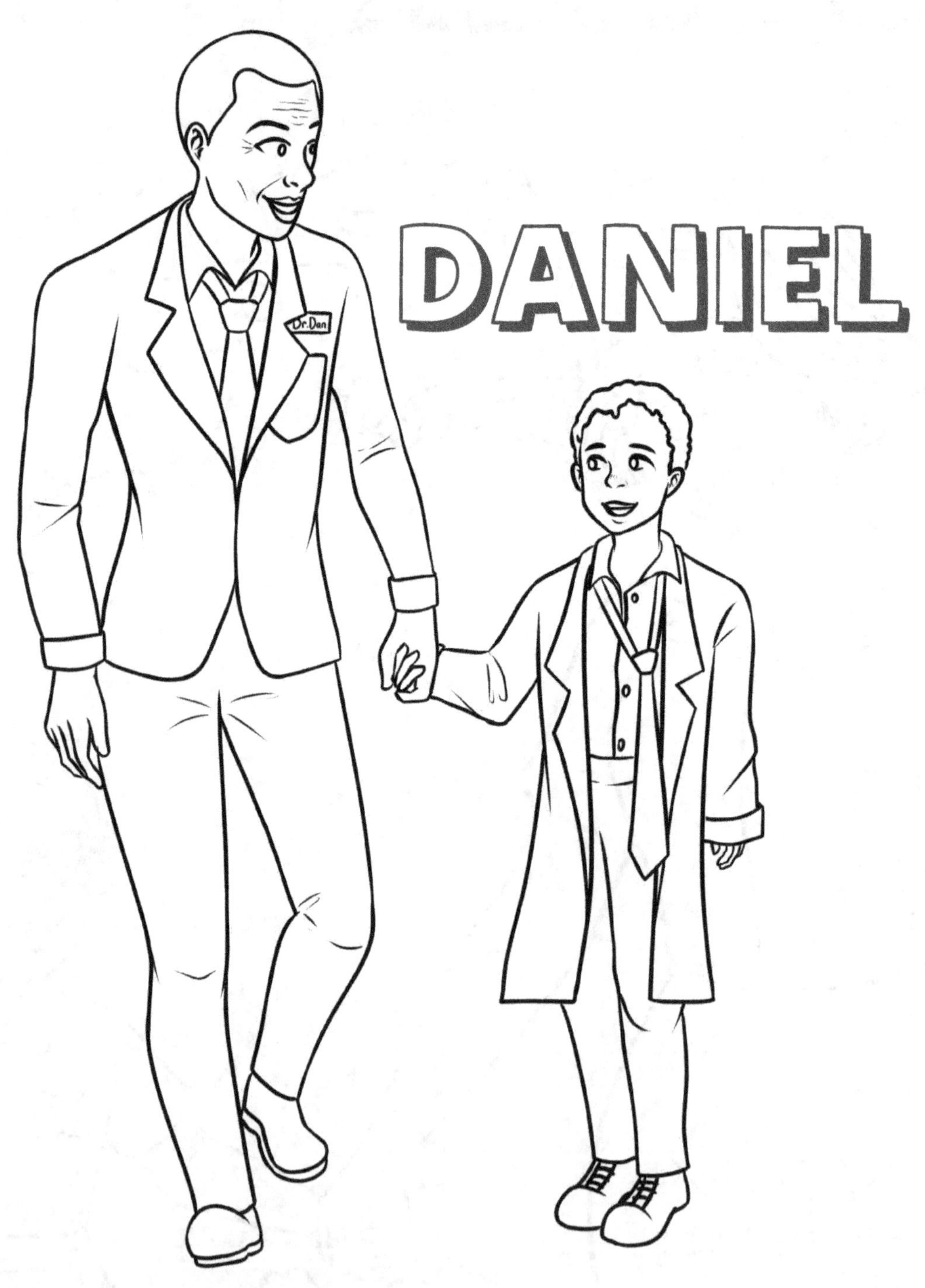

DANNY

HAPPY INDEPENDENCE DAY

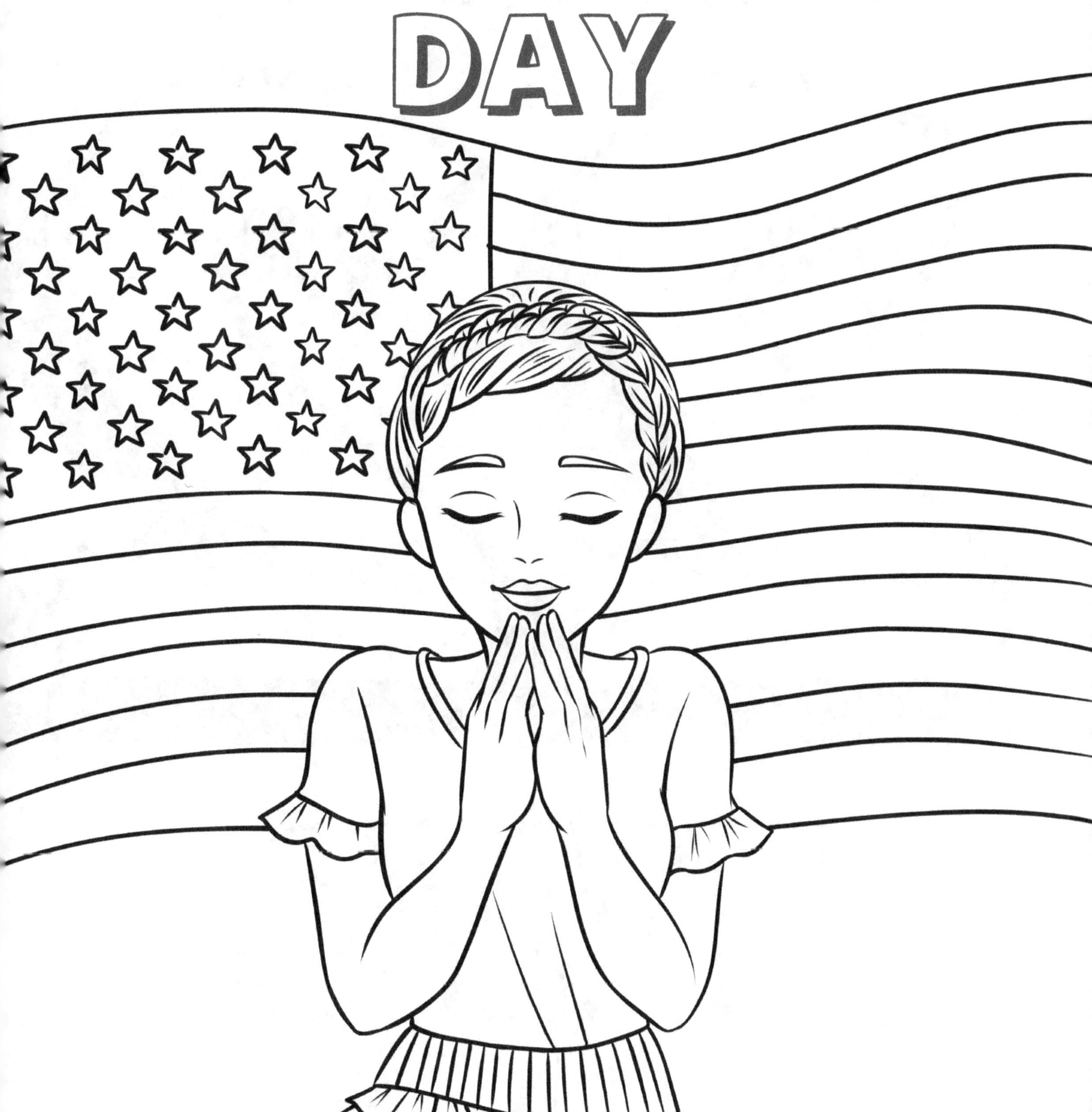

TWO

22

TWO

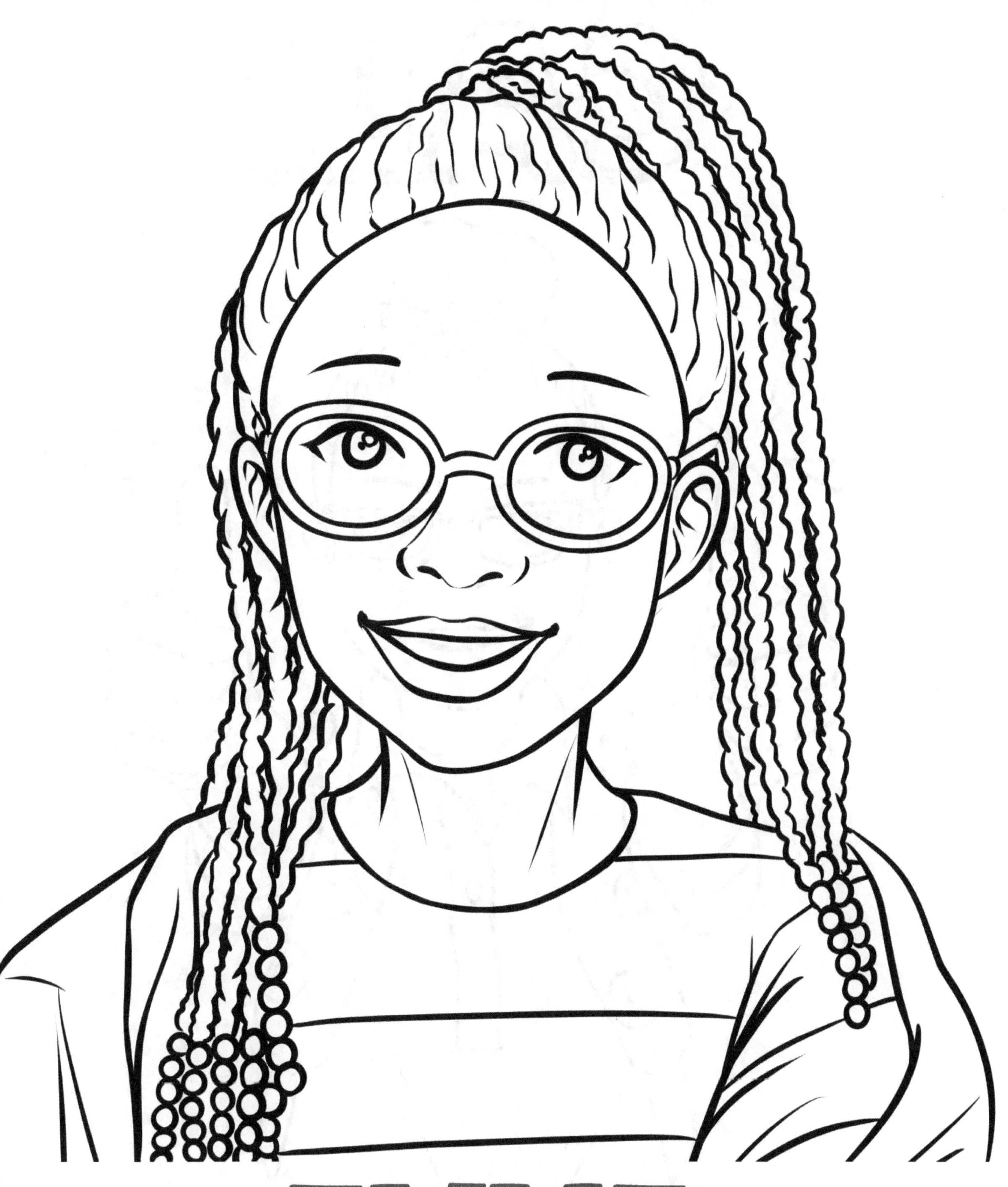

EVYE

CALI

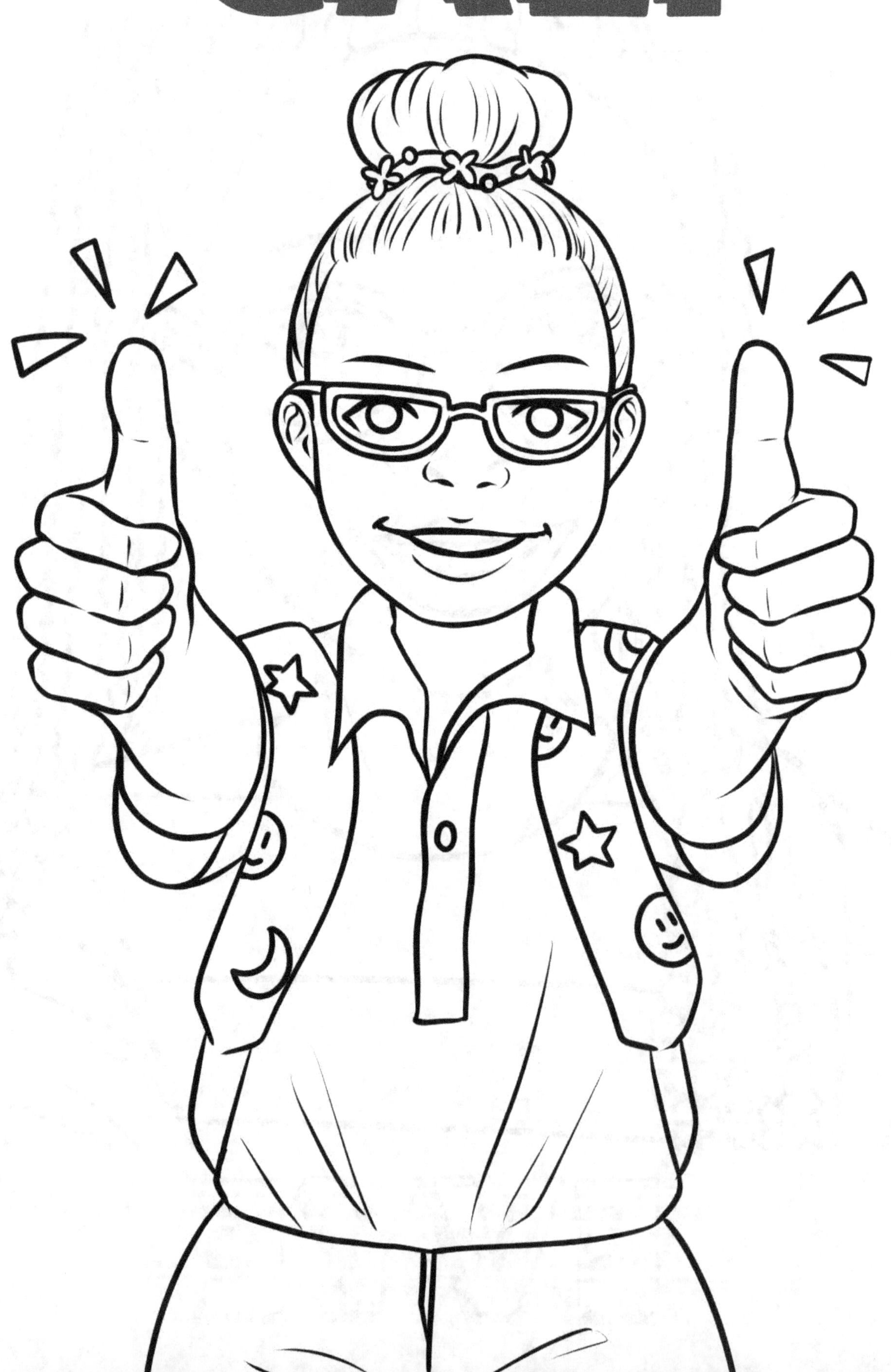

ELLINGTON

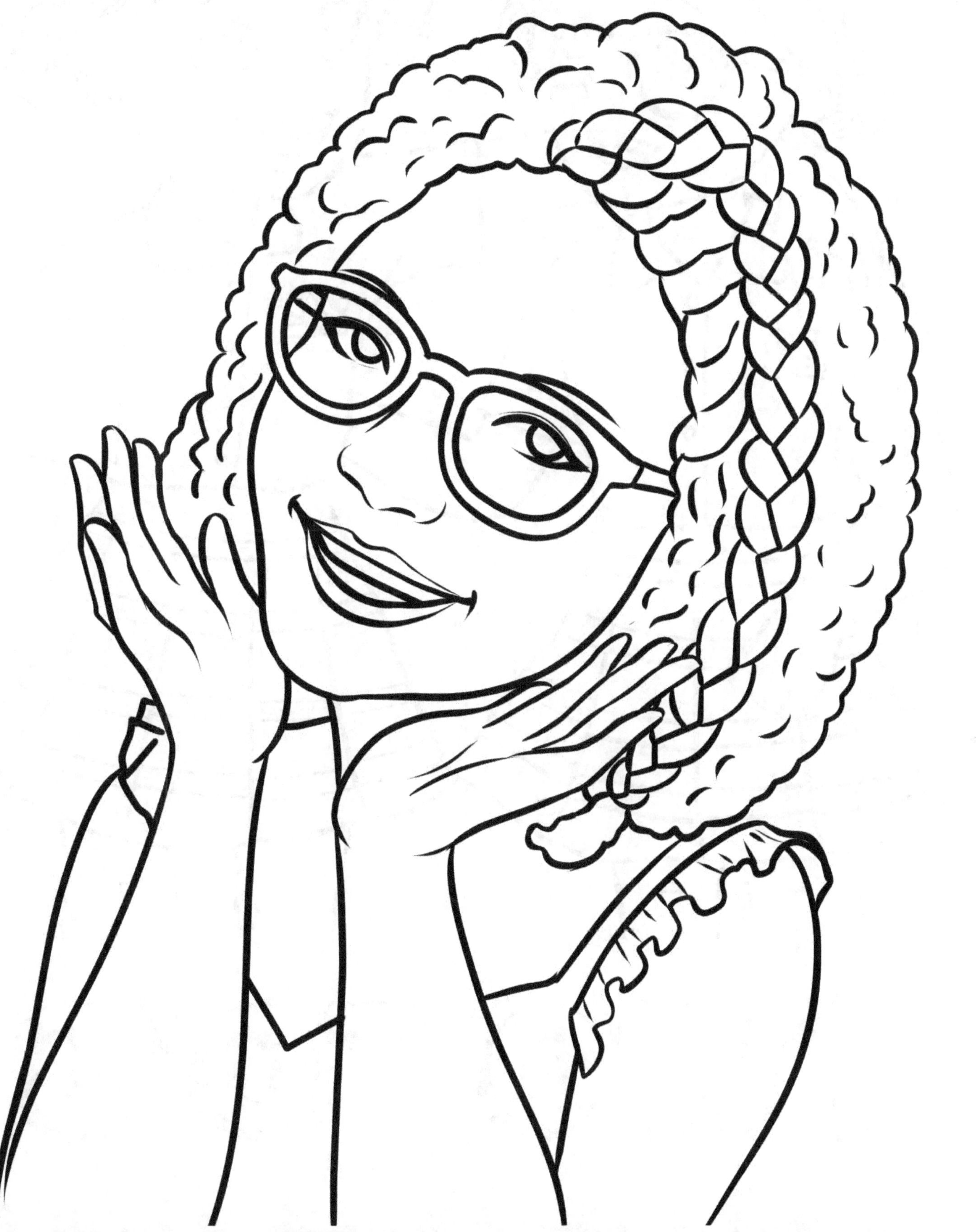

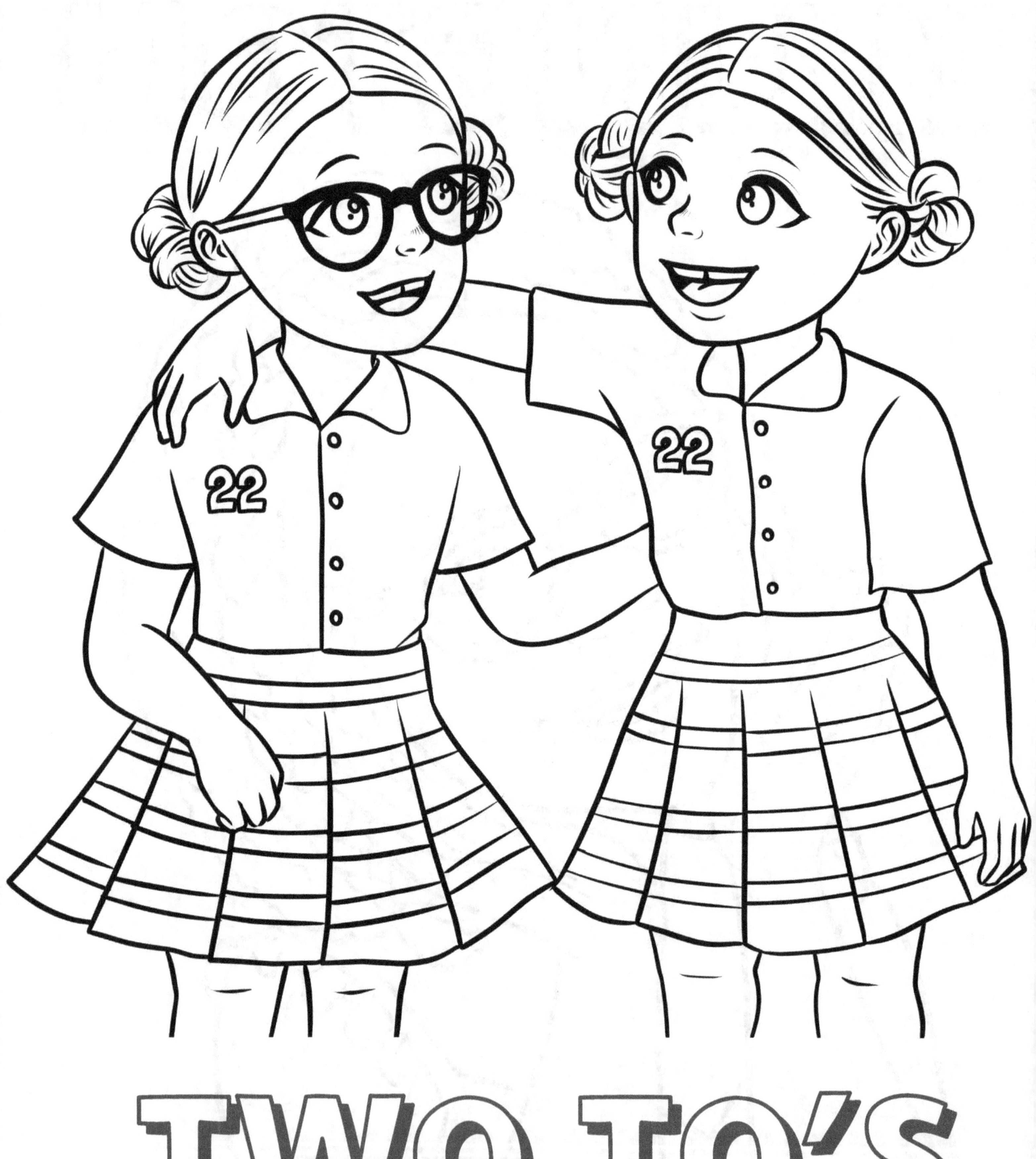

TWO TO'S

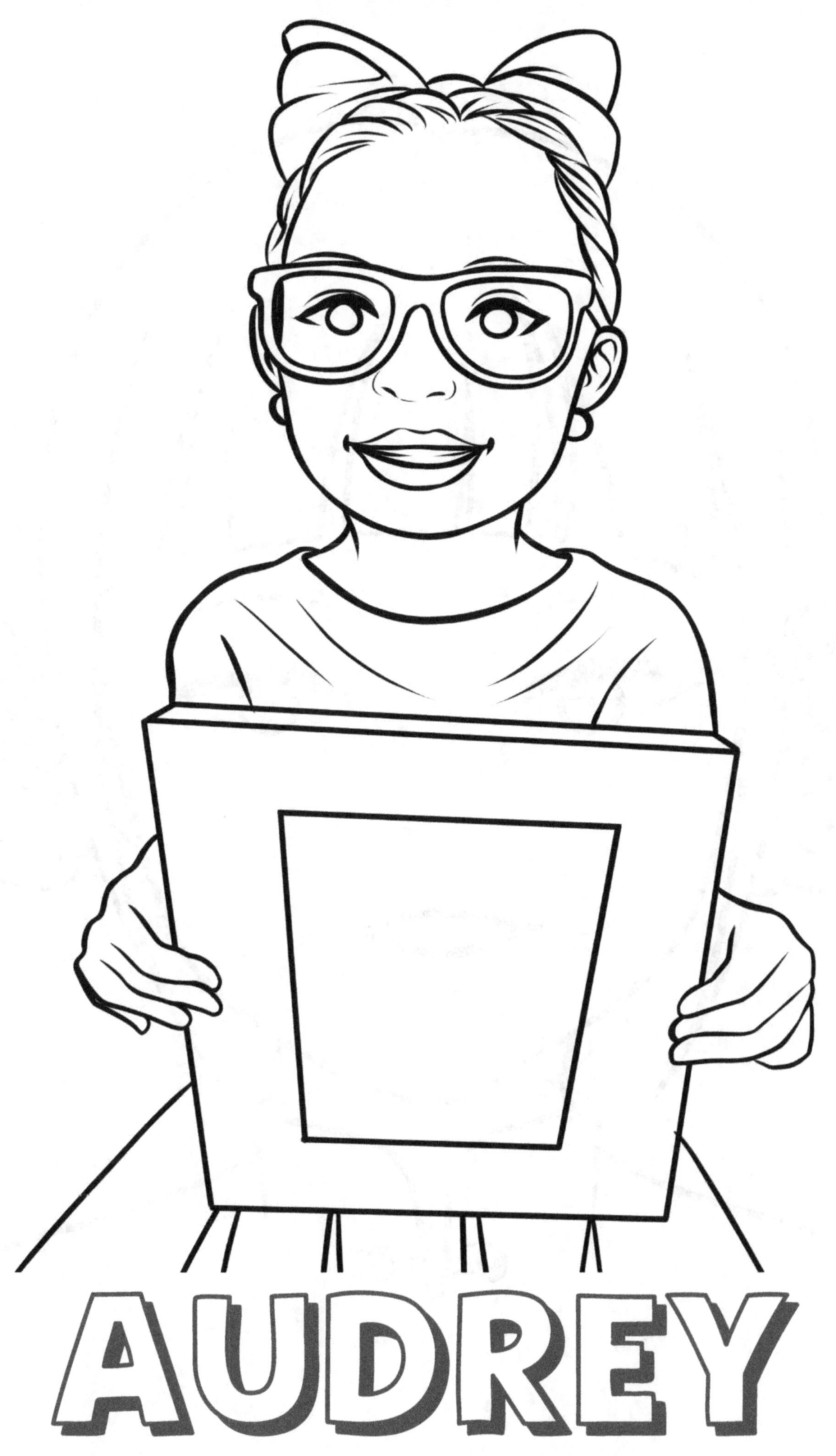
AUDREY

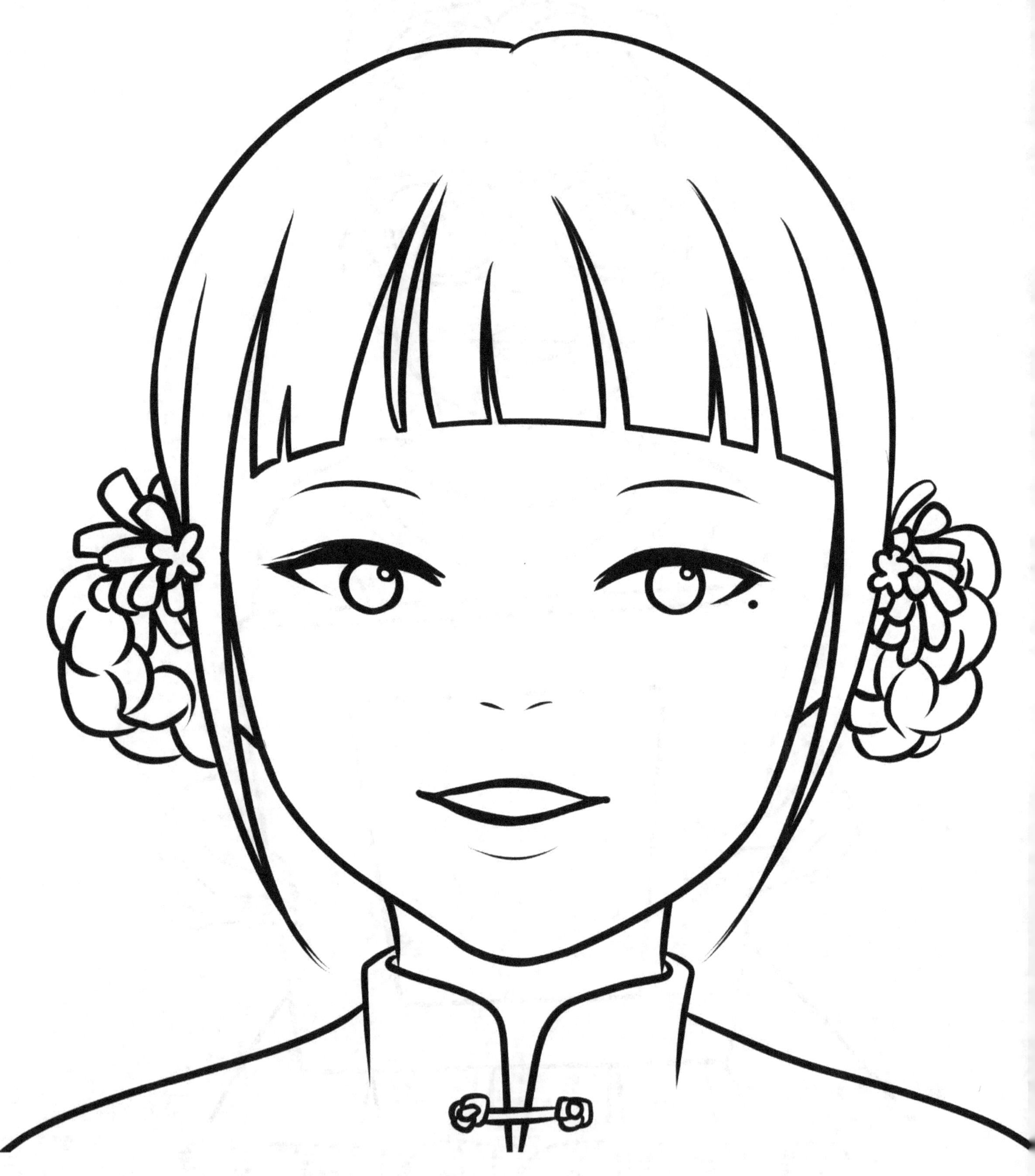

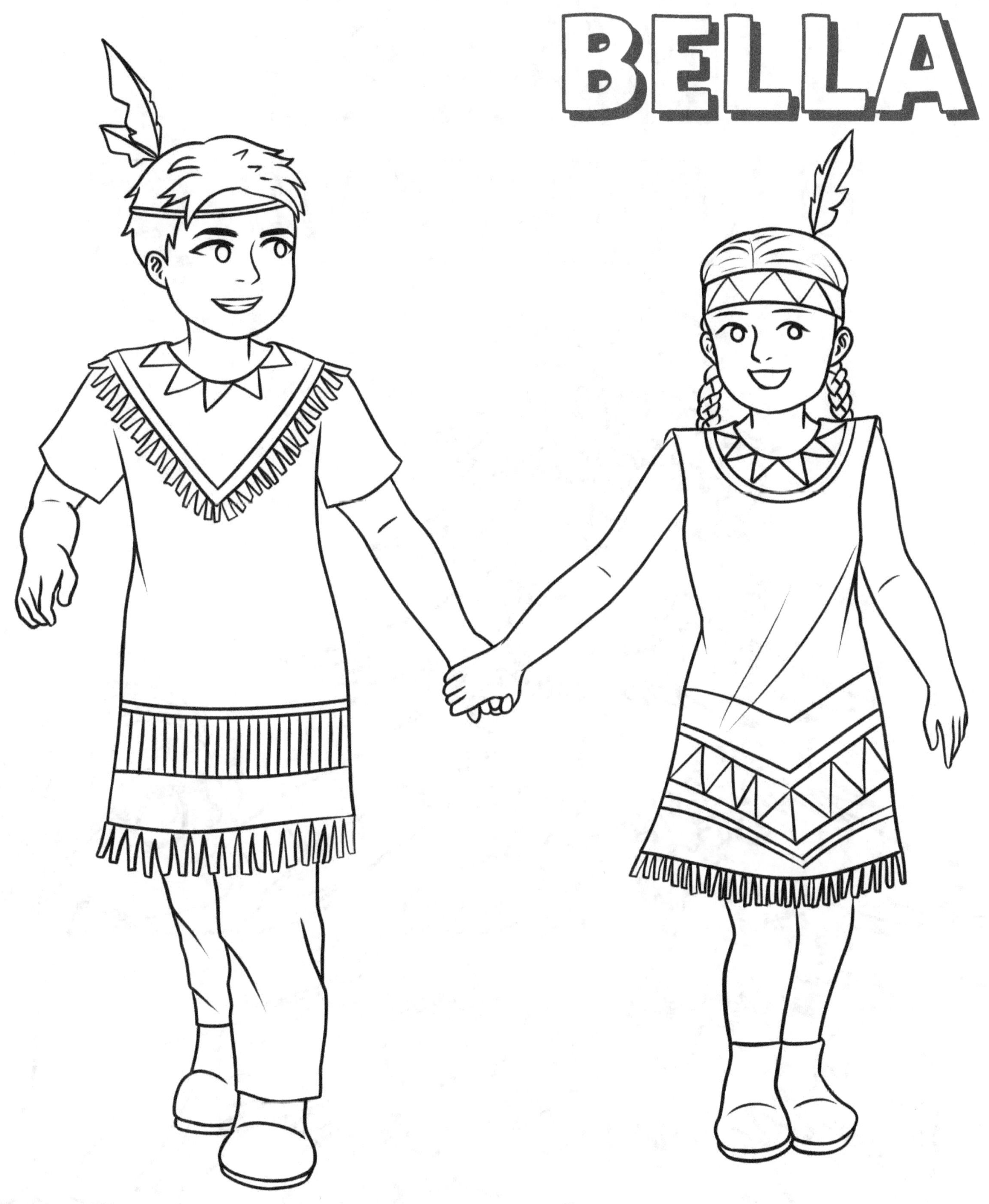
BELLA
CARTER

MERRY CHRISTMAS

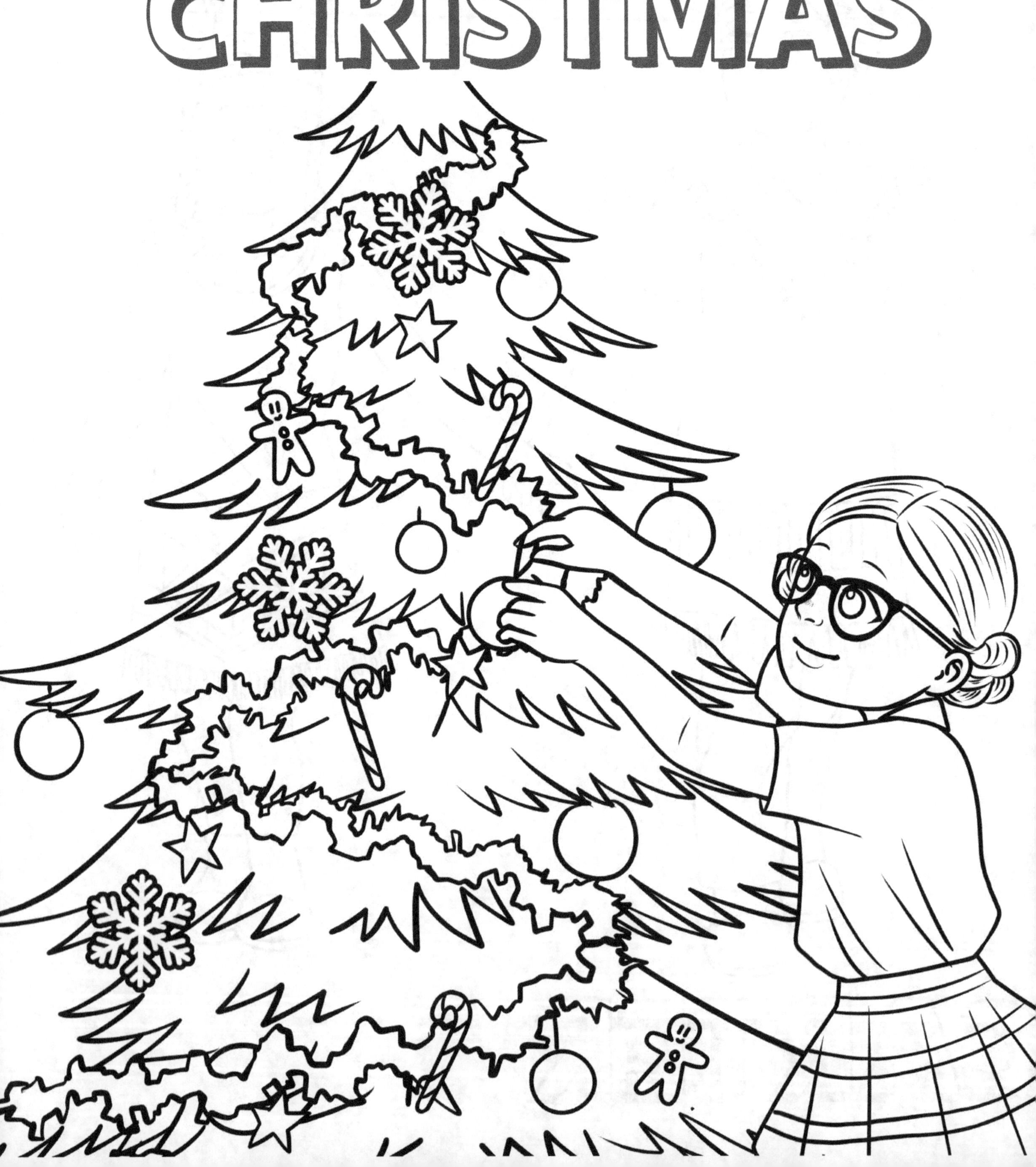

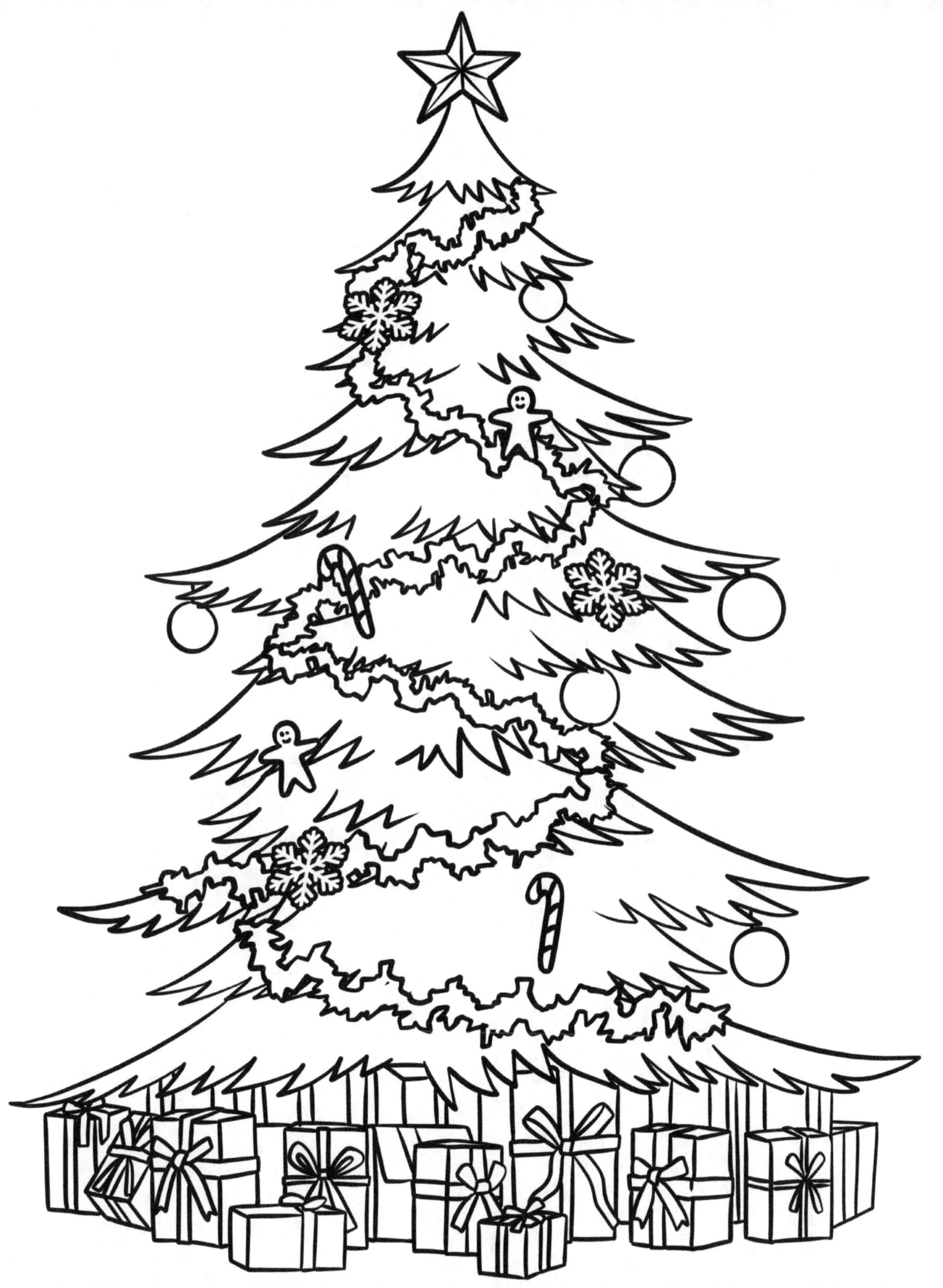

www.ingramcontent.com/pod-product-compliance
Lightning Source LLC
Chambersburg PA
CBHW082244060726
47598CB00016B/2772